Sand and Sea Breezes

Crystal McKenzie

Presentation by *BookLeaf Publishing*

Web: www.bookleafpub.com

E-mail: info@bookleafpub.com

ISBN: 978-93-95755-37-5

First edition 2022

This book has been dedicated to my father Rory Bradbury, my best friend Kaela as well as my amazing friend Dave.

ACKNOWLEDGEMENT

I would like to thank my friends Bianca, Emily, Joey and Joss from Thetis Island for inspiring me to get back into my love for poetry and sharing in my passion for creative writing. I would also like to acknowledge the Thetis Island community for inspiring me ever day and welcoming me to this wonderful paradise you all call home. Thank you to Bookleaf Publishing for posting the 21-everyday writing challenge on Facebook and giving me this amazing opportunity to take the next step in my passion for poetry.

PREFACE

Sand and Sea Breezes is my first written book of original poetry. I have always felt a need and want to express my feelings for longing with love in a creative way. I was inspired to write this book while I spent a year out on one of the most beautiful Southern Gulf Islands in British Columbia called Thetis Island. The quiet isolation of this small friendly community was everything I needed in my life at that time. Being surrounded by the ocean every day gave me a newfound sense of purpose and peace within myself. Watching the otters, hearing the sea birds and seeing the occasional seal and whale made this experience a once-in-a-lifetime opportunity for me. I would write most of my poems while watching passing sailboats through the restaurant window at the Marina where I worked. The peaceful environment of my surroundings made every day inspirational and the people I would meet from all walks of life filled my day with many new poetry ideas.

Have You Ever

Have you ever had a feeling you couldn't shake
A memory you couldn't erase, sweet lonely
heartbreak
Now I will be catching a case of feelings for you
Out the door too, shut them down for you
Hot summer sun having fun, is where it all
begun
Sail on the breeze, weakness in my knees
Holding hands in the sand making memories
All these bad choices knowing I'm only hoping
Never let me down before and now I'm rolling
Blueberry bud in my blunt, trying to smoke you
away
Guess I will just sit with these feelings
Blow them away, another rainy day
Each drop reminds me of how bitter it tastes
Sour like a lemon yet sweet like a treat
Mixed emotions over you, never missing a beat
Could never tell if it was you or me
Missing something we never had
How bittersweet
The thought of loving you had my mind at ease
Yet hoping only knowing your miles at sea
That's how you wanted it to be
Do you ever think of me, or am I wasting all my
time and energy

Soulmates is what I thought we could be
Our connection was so strong, solid concrete
All smiles and laughs is where it all started
Found out I was taken, now your dearly
departing
I am the one to blame, I just love too much
Just another day of never getting what our hearts
truly want
Have you ever

Left Unsaid

Every time I think I have something to say
I sit in silence and smoke it all away
At times it makes me forget all the thoughts in
my head
Yet I imagine all the things I have left unsaid
I should have told you how much love I felt for
you
The brightness of your smile made me feel
brand new
You were always the sunset in my grey skies
Yet all this love I feel is withering and dying
inside
I want to tell you all my stories, my dreams and
all my hopes
I envision you meeting my family the ones I
hold dear to my heart so close
Remembering the wetness of my tears and the
fears of losing you
A battle inside which I will always lose
Every time I think of writing to you with
something to say
My hands get sweaty and I start to shake
I don't understand why I feel this way
I scream speak up, let the truth breathe

Yet I dive into my journal, let my secrets out on
every page
Until I can figure out this maze
I will sit in silence and blow you away
And with each intake of air, my body takes
I will remind myself of all the things I have left
unsaid

Self Sabotage

I don't know why I always do this to myself
You would think time after time I would ask for
some help
Instead, I sit in silence and contemplate to
myself
Should I really love you while loving someone
else
Is my heart too big and my head too small
Feeling these thoughts distract me from it all
The fact is, what I feel feels so wrong
I can't quite seem to shake this off
These memories of you floating in my head
To the most obtrusive, lying next to you while I
lay awake in my own bed
Enough said, I have had more than enough
Self Sabotage is always a must, broken trust
Beating myself down for loving the two of you
Married once and for a lifetime
Yet you surprised me out of the blue
Met you in the summer gave a smile and a wave
From that day I could not erase your name from
my brain
Your presence met mine, claimed twin flame
You never knew me and were just playing the
game

Of charisma and charm, swept me off my feet
Still don't know how you really felt about me
So many feelings and thoughts left unsaid
Eats me alive knowing and only hoping
That what you meant to me was more than a
small moment
In time with you, watching my soul peer right
through
To the core of your soul
How my thoughts and feelings spin out of
control
Not just my mind, I feel restless in my bones
What's it to you, I don't expect you to care
As I was always taken
Must have been love in the air
Walking away without any cares
Just more broken promises to myself
How dare I doubt there could ever be someone
else
Self sabotage

Willow Bend

I can feel the wind beneath my feet
My roots are deep and endless
The force of air makes my branches bend
Never the strength to be broken
I hear a voice now on the breeze
Silently whispering to me
Sweet words fill my ears, grey skies in my eyes
As the rain from above soaks my leaves
Drenching and cleansing my core, the purity of
finding an old soul
I never thought I could miss you so much more
Caught it early this time, felt from the bottom up
Never shakeable, almost breakable
Always bending with the flow
Grounded at the base, leaves twirl and fill the
sky
I still stand tall, remain strong, Oak and Pine
For this is a reflection of the love of you and I

No More Secrets

Let's be honest, you and I
We both want what we have to deny
At first, I knew my slick and sly
Told a person here and there
Hoping you would find
The unsettling truth which I chose to hide
I can't believe I have lived with such fear
This is my whole damn life
No more secrets, let's clear the air
Friends are forever, you are my favorite friend
I chose today to love you until the very end
You bring my life joy with each reply
Yet I hide with my truth in darkness, at times I
deny
Deny my feelings hope to breathe
Deny my love knowing it hurts you and me
You never were a secret, everybody knew
Chemistry and soul connection
Is what brought me to you
You showed me kindness, when I hated myself
You were that smile that I needed
When I was drowning, saving myself
You would be that joke, just to hear me laugh
Your actions showed me what I was truly
missing

The way I wanted and needed to be treated
Yet I sit in silent chaos, stuck and never
changing
Today I choose to let it all be
You're the friend my soul desperately needs
No more indecision, time to be brave
If he has questions, I will stand strong in my
ways
Favorite friend I will defend my case
Even if I fall apart at the seams and break
Just lend a hand, help me up
I will be strong enough to dust myself off
I tip my hat to you, I landed quite well
Throw this lucky coin of mine into the wishing
well
No more secrets

My Favorite Friend

It went so well the first week and two
We got real with each other
Learned about love as we grew
I told you some things I thought would be too
much
Yet you turned around and said you needed me
as such
I took your hand and walked beside you
While you held my hand knowing you had to let
go
Now I feel fearless with so much rage to show
We knew this wasn't going to last forever
We both knew how difficult it would be
Now we play the game where we are both too
busy
Avoid our honest chats, what happened
That made it all end in a flash
Was it clarity or the reality of us setting in
We could never have each other with the
situation I was in
It didn't hold me back and you were too in love
to care
Now I am standing here watching it all
disappear
I am not angry today, knowing you won't reply

You drew lines in the sand and clearly stated
We are friends, just you and I
I wanted to cry, shed my tears over nothing
As there was never really anything there
Just the air and space between us
Which you read between all the lines
The way I go about it
I know it's what changed your mind
I just needed to know I was never too much to
handle
My love is no easy task
Too large to hold, too wild to tame
Yet you can always sail in and take my breath
away
Without my breath I still feel you near
You're the only vision that clouds all my
judgment
Yet with you I love with no attachment
That's why it was never hard to watch you go
You will always be my favorite friend
Like the tide let go and flow
Leave it to the power of the universe
Only in time will she show, what is truly meant
to be
One day I will be with you and you with me
Sandy beaches and sun-kissed skin
Only until then will I imagine it

Sail Away

I never thought it would end like this
Your eyes and smile is what I will miss
The sheer sparkle in your gaze
Yet I doubt you even know my name
It is rare to find someone
Who makes me feel like you do
A moth to your flame is what I am to you
Or do you feel the same
I will never know
Just like the ocean, ebb and flow
I roll with the tides life chooses to bring
Maybe it was the summer-induced haze
Take my memory with you and my known name
Take the pieces of my heart and keep sailing
away

Amongst The Waves

They say you're a lost cause
I couldn't care less
I have been a hero to many
Never rest, always blessed
You never needed to be saved
Just rescued from yourself
When our eyes first met I knew
You had found yourself
You nestled in my presence
Your energy met mine
A match made for the heavens
Love is always blind
I swear we could have been the perfect pair
Not now, the time is not right
Maybe we can try again in the next life
Until then carry the pieces of my heart with you
I am never too far, no matter where you are
Lay your head and gently listen
Hear that sound
Crashing waves, feeling the bright sun rays
Is where we can be found

The Compassion Key

Compassion blessed us with her grace
I held back every compulsion
You knew I could not fake
Feelings were all over my face
You stand in your brilliance
Tell me see you next week
My whole body numbs
I feel my knees go weak
The butterflies in my stomach have reached new
peaks
What is this spell, the witchery you have caused
These feelings are real without cause
Do you believe in soulmates
I certainly do
Compassion was the key
That led me straight to you

Forever And Eternally

I sit quietly and feel your stare
In the warmth of your loving gaze
Grace fills the air
I try my best to refrain and ignore
The love of your never giving touch
My hands shake and tremble
So I lock them in my lap
My gaze upon you is all you need
To know how much both our souls needed to be
seen
Your soul, my soul forever and eternally

Orange Aroma

You stepped in off the beach
Sandy hair blowing in the breeze
The color of the sea sparkled from your eyes
Reminding me of your smile, so sweet
Like the rind of an orange, blazing and bright
Your soul had met mine that night, tropical
delight
You sailed away that summer
Leaving me bitterly, my heart exploded
Cut thinly sliced, through and through
All I can do now is sit here
Drinking in my feelings about you
When I feel that summer sea breeze
The smooth sand beneath my feet
I hope you always remember
The orange juice, I drink and drink

Somber Speech

I feel the melancholy creeping in
My window left open, all rushing in
A cloud, strange mist if you must
Swirls around the room on every wall
That is enough
Now dust on the floor is what I have left
Chirp chirp at the sill, turn my head to the
window
Smile and see my fellow sparrow
He took flight, what a sight
A blessing with broken wings
What sound was that chirp
Heard first on the breeze
Closing my eyes to finally get some rest
Sit up, walk slowly to the window
That I forgot open and left

Slowly Growing

What to do when your stuck in a moment
Can't catch your breath, nothing controlling
Let go of the reins, I am stuck in between
What I find peaceful and ultimate rage
Leave love out of this one there is no room
Quiet thoughts I must speak out loud
Held truth, I can feel my blood boil
Calmly I sit
Is this why we are truly meant to exist
Experience each moment, each breath
While calmly sitting, yet you feel like your
spinning
Unforgiving
Not out of control, well within reach
Planted down, boulder to crown
Your motion in moment is where I can be found
Standing tall, rising slowly
Peace within your soul
Slowly growing

Winter Snow

Yesterday the sun was bright in the sky
The warmth brought out every freckle on my
face
This morning I walked in snow covered hills
Frozen in the moment, missing you still
Knowing with each breath I let go
Like the falling of the cold snow
To need you like the sun
Yet love you like the snow
We learned to let each other go
Just know, in another lifetime
We would sail away
Dance with our shadows in the moonlight
To know without knowing
The smell of your hair, the softness of your skin
Only in my mind do I create our paradise
Like the changing of each season when it begins

Unlock My Mind

Keep your mind open
Love with all your heart
It was the way I was raised
All I have been taught
I move through the flows of life
Going up and coming down
Smiling when I am happy
Feeling down with a frown
Some people understand me
Within a few days or upon gaze
Some it takes years to remember a name
With you it was different
You saw straight through
My energy melted right into you
I don't need your love
Affection or attention
Just a smile and a wave, simple blessings
Even though when your not near
I close my eyes and see you there
Standing tall, a key in your hand
As you come and go I feel the warmth in demand
You love without judgment
That is what I admire most
My mind wanders with you, wherever you go
Yet my thoughts never travel too far
For you have the key to my mind and my heart

Timeless: Sand Down

Time is just something
I always fall short of
Yet the one thing I need is time for myself
Blessed to have friends
To lend an ear, be that rock
As I alone am on this path to discover
Discover you say, what could I find
Let me free fly in this spiral
Diamonds for eyes, skin made of glass
A faint glowing ember where the heart lay
Fire for hair and a pearly white smile
I saw this creature, stayed a long while
Scared do you say, not me, not now, not never
Sitting in silence watching the glow
I knew this creature from my head to my toes
Gently I floated up out of that spiral
To realize the creature was me
Just like sand in an hourglass, hit bottom and flip
More sand down, I am timeless

Don't Wait For Me

I've been here before
I don't want to do this to you
As I have done to him time and time again
Please don't wait for me
It's never fair
You know I have wanted to be with you
From the gaze of your first stare
You saw the fire in my eyes
My heart upon my sleeve
Yet I am the one that has done
The damage to make you bleed
Please don't wait for me
I dream about you more than I care to share
Sometimes I wonder if you meet me there
In the chaos of our minds, dream on if you
please
Bewildered by each other, knowing when to
freeze
You walked away with my soul
As my hand was with another
Complicated this will always be
Our friendship is where we left it
Both yearning for each other's midnight screams
Please don't wait for me
I would never take advantage of your patience

Or the kindness and joy you bring to my grey
skies
Underneath it all are feelings I can't deny
Everyday this love grows stronger
And it breaks my heart to know
Do you feel the same about me, or can you
watch me as I go
Don't hold your breath to long and become light
headed
Walking hand in hand along the sandy beaches
Hoping one day we have the chance
To be the real us, beyond what is past
Just know the pain I have inflicted
Doesn't make me feel any better than the rest
Please don't wait for me
You have been hurt before
Not by the games I know I choose to play
So instead of waiting, just walk away
Leave it all behind
Our memory is with the waves
Hear the ocean crash and the midnight moon
howl
Let our love for each other live on
The breeze of the sea, calmly rolling
And when you see that seagull in the sky, don't
cry
Take a moment and reminisce
Of all we could have been within our bliss
Please don't wait for me

Picture On The Wall

Sometimes I wonder
If my picture is on your wall
Do you remember that summer
I do, we both fell so hard
Landed on our feet at best
Never knowing each other's names, let's guess
I had to remember you by the color of your eyes
and the kindness in your smile
I am thankful that you would stop in
Every once in awhile
You thought the same way about me and my
bambi brown eyes
You saw the sadness in my fake forced smile
Your charm and compassion that day
Broke through the ice that surrounded my heart
Yet you were not in fright, great delight
You stared into my soul that day
Lit my body with your desire
I will not forget the sea breeze to cool me down
As you know that's what I had admired most
I was drowning in your passion
For love, peace and compassion
Now the summer has passed and fall is upon us
I still have your penthouse view framed
Not on the wall, yet as a memory in my mind

I still hope you have that picture of me
That I purposefully left behind, closed frame
Hang it high for all your friends to see
So we can both remember that summer
From the heights up above
Just know I am always with you, always and
forever
In a frame as a picture
Always lit up by good weather

Everyday Moments

I wish you were there with me
Watching every wave roll in
Sitting on the dock watching passing sails
Hearing every seagull as we watch them in the
sky
I am blessed that you taught me to love
In everday moments
When he walked in and took my breath away
Oh how I wish you could have seen
The happiest smile upon my face
He was full of charm, passion and grace
I am blessed that you taught me to love
In everyday moments
I had conversations with the wise and lonely
The old and the young
People from near and far
They taught me to be free and worry so much
less
I could see you in every person I met
I am blessed that you taught me to love
In everyday moments
When I had to leave paradise behind
Know that only for a moment I cried
The tears came and then flowed away like the
rising and lowering of the tide

I was calm and knew this was the way it had to
be
I said my goodbyes to the sand, the sails and the
sea
Made room in my heart for all those I chose to
keep
I am thankful for all who inspired me to be
The best version of myself while on this journey
by the sea
I am blessed that you taught me to love
In everyday moments

Soul Friend

I will love you when my heart has healed
Been washed with coarse sea sand
I will hope to return to you
Upon the wings of singing sea birds as they land
Find my kindness in the cool ocean breeze
Count our blessings on every star above
This love I have hidden deep
No diver will ever think of
For the ocean is much too fathom
Our friendship will last a lifetime
How can you see right through
Like my soul is made of sea glass
Yet I can see your soul clear through
We are looking through colorful shards
That are smooth and in shades of blue, green and
sometimes hues of red
Our souls met upon that island in the quiet calm
of night
To be instantly intertwined
Underneath that full moon light, standing by the
tide
I knew we would be soul friends until the end of
time
The water makes the sea run deep
Each wave brings life to its depths

The sand so gracefully awaits the shore hoping
to be blessed
Starfish, crabs and shells galore the beauty and
treasures you can find
Just like when you hold my hand
Let our frienship be the treasure we both hold
For others to be inspired to find a soul friend of
their own
The beauty of the island is worth the treasures it
beholds
Together just like sand and sea my soul friend
you will always be

Sand and Sea Breezes

I hope you hear my heartbeat when you put that
shell up to your ear
Remember all our times together as we lay up on
the sand
When the crashing and the rolling of the waves
cause deep peace within
I hope you can remember all the passion we can
bring
To our lives and to each other, this we can not
doubt
So look above and hear and feel the sound of
every gull
As they glide through the sky on the salty breeze
When you have a chance please remember me
Sit up on the dock and watch the sunset glow
Dip your toes into the tide and feel the power of
the flow
When you miss me wish upon every star you see
As the sky is always clear and we will always be
One with each other like the sand and sea
breezes
Being with you in each small passing moment
Take your boat upon the waves
I will watch you as you sail
When you reach your final destination

Enjoy the journey and the comfort of the warmth
For we will always be the calm before the storm
No matter how far apart, I will be the raging sea
You I can always find upon the cool sea breeze
So let us walk amongst the sand and enjoy this
ocean view
Watch the otters splash about, reach down and
touch a starfish or two
While we love each other in this moment
Let it not slip us by
Lay here with me upon the sand and hear our
souls ask why
Why can't this love last forever between you and
I
Yet we will always be around for the ocean does
not sleep and the sand can make its depths even
at the bottom of the sea
So take our love and place it, bury it in the sand
Let the sea breeze blow and take it to a foreign
land
Our love will last forever upon the new found
shore
Always remember we can find ourselves
In the love we buried deep, safe and sound
Along the sand with the cool sea breezes

9 789395 755375